THE FORD TRANSIT STORY

THE FORD TRANSIT STORY

GILES
CHAPMAN

Published in the United Kingdom in 2011 by
The History Press
The Mill · Brimscombe Port · Stroud · Gloucestershire · GL5 2QG

British Library Cataloguing in Publication Data
A catalogue record for this book is available from the British
Library.

Hardback ISBN 978-0-7524-6283-7

Typesetting and origination by The History Press
Printed in China

CONTENTS

The phrase 'white van man' is one that's familiar to everyone in Britain and, what's more, we all have a pretty accurate idea of what it implies. White van man is aggressive, loud, pressed for time, and just a little bit lax about vehicle maintenance and cleaning. If he isn't running his own small business, playing one customer off against another to keep several 'jobs' going at once, then he's a road warrior on a company fleet, pounding the tarmac for hours on end to deliver the goods and get his shift over.

Who first coined the tabloid-friendly tag will probably never be known. Early-morning BBC Radio 2 mainstay Sarah Kennedy certainly helped to popularise it from 1997; she had white van men across Britain, firing up their trusty steeds, as her audience, after all, so it was as much a term of endearment as a mild insult.

In 2011, moreover, BBC Three began airing a sitcom called *White Van Man* – the calamitous, and pretty funny, exploits of an odd-job man battling to make a crust. Its producers knew there could be only one vehicle to take a starring role. A white van, obviously, but it couldn't be anything other than a Ford Transit.

The Transit has been a part of the British way of life for nearly five decades. There were plenty of vans before the Transit but none met the demands of so many different users in such a perfect way. The Transit set new benchmarks of usability, durability and versatility. It transformed the task of driving a van from handling a piece of industrial machinery to an experience much closer to using a conventional car.

It somehow did this with a ballsy, stylish, go-getting character – very much

Nose-to-nose across six decades: the 1965 original on the right squares up to the very latest Ford Transit.

the light commercial vehicle counterpart of the nippy Escort, the chunky Cortina and the satisfying Capri that helped make Ford a best-selling byword for customer satisfaction.

And, would you believe, the Transit also did its bit to make Europe a more harmonious place – and even taught the mighty Mercedes-Benz a thing or two. No, really! Here comes the story of the Ford Transit.

The arrival of the very first Ford in Europe was in 1903, four years before the debut of the seminal Model T, when two Ford Model As were freighted from New York to London. They were proudly exhibited in Westminster's Royal Agricultural Hall the following year. Then, in 1911, Manchester welcomed Ford's first-ever assembly plant outside the USA. In a few short years, there were similar satellites in Germany, France, Spain and Italy; the British, German and French operations, though, would evolve, by degree, to become proper European car and truck manufacturers that created their own vehicles from scratch, rather than bolting them together from kits of parts.

We take globalisation as a given now, but throughout the first half of the twentieth century each country was an economic fortress. Trading between nations was conducted from behind a rampart of protective currency and import restrictions. This was why Henry Ford was unable to flood the world market with his cheap and rugged Model Ts; in the main, he was only granted access to countries if the cars could be assembled or manufactured locally so that jobs would be created and currency wouldn't be sucked back to the USA.

It led to the weird situation, in the mid-1950s, of Ford companies in Germany and Britain (the French one had been sold in 1954) making ranges of cars in which virtually no parts were the same. In Britain, we had our Popular, Anglia, Consul and Zephyr/Zodiac while in Germany there was a range of Taunus models. Some of the smaller-engined cars both used a very old design of 1172cc sidevalve engine. That was about all the commonality there was.

Mass-production guru Henry Ford with his car that put the world on wheels, the Ford Model T.

One thing the two European Ford companies did share increasingly, however, was an American-influenced desire to give their car buyers great value and innovative design. The tight focus on serving the customer began with the MkI Consul/Zephyr range in 1951, the first production car with stable, pliant MacPherson strut suspension and the first Ford with unitary construction. The lively Anglia 105E followed in 1959 with Ford's first four-speed gearbox, and by the early 1960s the motorway-friendly Ford Cortina had arrived in Britain and Germany's equivalent, the Taunus 12M, offered the twin novelties of front-wheel drive and a compact V4 engine.

Simultaneous to all this showroom activity, a single European market had tentatively taken shape.

◄ *Model T vans fulfilled an infinite number of roles, some of which – like this danger-fraught scenario – the Health & Safety Executive would have a fit about today.*

◄◄ *The very first vehicle off the production line at Ford's brand new Dagenham plant in 1931 was a light commercial vehicle, a Model A pick-up.*

◄ *Launched in 1948 in the USA but never exported to Britain, Ford's robust F Series pick-ups were an amazing success, selling 110,000 in that year alone.*

On 1 January 1958 the European Economic Community's (EEC) Common Market officially began as the trade barriers between Germany, France, Belgium, Holland, Italy and Luxembourg were swept away by the Treaty of Rome. At the same time, the other European countries not participating, which numbered Britain, Sweden, Denmark, Norway, Austria, Switzerland and Portugal, banded together to become the European Free Trade Association (EFTA), a little looser politically but still opening up markets for each others' goods.

Believe me, I never set out to deliver an economics lecture in this book, but the last few paragraphs help to explain where Ford found itself shortly before it began work on the Transit. It was either this or a spiel about the history of delivering cardboard boxes in vans, so you've got off lightly.

Anyway, the upshot was that Ford entered the 1960s with a stake in the EEC and the EFTA. This would be taxing for company bosses sitting around the boardroom table in Detroit. Ford of Britain enjoyed massive success in its home market with great cars like the Anglia and Cortina, and the EFTA gave it 100m consumers to chase; Ford Germany, meanwhile, was a bit of a weakling in a home territory dominated by Volkswagen and Opel, yet the EEC gave it potential access to 200m consumers.

Passenger cars were one thing, but Ford was just as big in commercial vehicles, from the smallest car-derived delivery van to large articulated trucks. Once again, in its standard vans, there were two completely different European types.

Ford Germany introduced its FK1000 (it stood for Ford Köln, for Cologne, 1000, meaning its 1000kg payload) in 1953, as a direct response to the runaway success of the Volkswagen Transporter. Perhaps unsurprisingly, it looked pretty similar to the VW but underneath the boxy profile with the long front overhang, it was nothing like it. The water-cooled, four-cylinder Taunus engine was mounted between the front seats, to drive the rear wheels. Despite being offered with plenty of options, including sliding side doors, it was an unremarkable workhorse, but in the economic environment of the mid-1950s sales were decent enough. By 1961, a rebrand now had it as the Ford Taunus Transit but its popularity was feeble by comparison with its Volkswagen counterpart.

This FK/Taunus was never seen in the UK, as right-hand-drive production wasn't even considered. No, we had our own Ford van and – before poking fun at the Germans – it should be said that it was every bit as mundane.

This was the Ford Thames 400E. In 1957 it had replaced the old E83W model that had been around since 1938, and so was a massive improvement over that. Like Germany's FK1000, the 400E had its engine (a 1.7-litre from the Consul saloon) mounted in a mid position between the driver and passenger, who sat above the front wheels in a forward-control position and enjoyed the relative sophistication of coil-spring independent front suspension. It was offered in two payload capacities of 10/12 and 15cwt and the monocoque construction on top of a ladder-frame chassis meant the standard van could be adapted with a wide variety of bodywork options. If you're having trouble picturing one, then just think of the minibus Charlie Croker's gang used in the movie *The Italian Job*!

The 400E's most serious bugbear would only emerge some years after a customer bought one; it was a notorious rustbucket. But it was also narrow, uncomfortable, and apt to get hot inside with that engine next to the driver. Its side passenger and load doors were hinged, rather than sliding, and the gearbox was at first three-speed only.

As with most British vans of the 1950s, it got the job done in a tinny, minimalist way, but the market leader was the Bedford CA, which was a more comforting, bonneted design – and so ever so slightly more car-like – and had sliding side doors which made it handy for deliveries in narrow streets.

Two corporate cultures in two countries, two vehicle ranges, two markets; it all seemed like wasteful madness to Ford chiefs in the USA. The barmy duplication could not continue, and so in 1961, as an experiment, Ford took the momentous decision to force its British and German outposts to collaborate on the design of one new vehicle that they could both sell.

During the 1950s, Ford was a force to be reckoned with in the lorry business, especially with its rugged, multi-use Thames Trader range.

17

FIRE TENDER

FORD MOTOR COMPANY LTD
DAGENHAM

◄◄ *Ford Germany's equivalent of the 400E was the FK1000, something of an also-ran beside the Volkswagen Transporter; this 1957 version is a Westfalia camper, clearly gunning for VW customers.*

◄ *The trusty but increasingly archaic E83W was Ford's staple light van right up until 1957.*

20

◄◄◄ *The Thames 400E arrived in 1957, purpose-designed as a van, i.e.: not car-derived, but offering the relative sophistication of independent front suspension.*

◄ *Bedford's CA was the market leader in light vans during the 1950s and early '60s. Drivers liked the engine up-front, the reasonably car-like characteristics, and the sliding doors.*

21

This groundbreaking joint-venture would be called Project Redcap, and a senior product planning executive called Ed Baumgartner was despatched to Europe to kick the project into action. After all, Ford had decided to sink a then enormous £10m into it. He was amazed at what he found. 'You can't imagine how separate the British and German organisations were when I came over from the USA to join the Redcap team at the end of 1961', he recalled. 'They didn't want to have anything to do with each other so my initial role was a combination of coach and referee. I had to step in and stop the bickering from time to time because the British loved teasing the Germans and the Germans loved teasing the British. There were times when it made co-ordinating a moonshot look the easiest thing in the world.'

Did You Know?

In 1968 12,000 Hertfordshire Scouts, their friends and parents saw the culmination of two years' frenzied collecting when they exchanged a wheelbarrow-load of two million Green Shield Stamps for a brand new Ford Transit minibus to donate to disabled children.

The brief that the warring factions finally settled down to was to replace both the Thames 400E and Taunus Transit with a single vehicle that would suit every market across Europe. All the usual, if non-specific, requirements were bandied about; that it must be tough, roomy, comfortable, cheap to operate and versatile enough to be adapted into all sorts of derivatives. But the multi-national Redcap engineers gave themselves some very specific criteria to meet.

The new van needed to be child's play to service – sounds like a no-brainer, of course, but almost all other vans had engines that were a pain in the neck to access, often buried deep under the cabin or requiring five components to be detached to get to the kaput one. That led on to the need for the design to be as simple as possible. And finally, with the arrival of the motorway age in Europe in the early 1960s, this van had to be easy and pleasant to drive. A pure load-lugger could never be quite as relaxing as a conventional car to punt

◄ A rough, early prototype of Ford's Project Redcap, photographed in 1964 while still undergoing gruelling pre-manufacture trials.

along all day at 60mph, or even negotiate twisty country lanes, but Redcap needed to be free of the unnerving handling vices that afflicted contemporary vans, especially when they were fully laden with cargo.

Arthur Molyneux was one of the British product planning team working on the initial market research who sought out Britain's small traders and fleet users to discover what really mattered to them. Naturally, they clamoured for the biggest payload within the tightest possible dimensions. As one of the building blocks of the design was a separate bonnet for easy mechanic access and to distance the driver from the engine, this meant the van would have to be either longer or wider to meet or beat its rivals. They plumped for wider.

Several senior executives in the company were rather perturbed at this, feeling a

◄◄ The interior of a 1965 pre-production Transit clearly showing the car-like accommodation made possible by having the engine ahead of the cabin.

◄ Wide-opening doors with an inbuilt step led on to the sort of commanding driving position that Transit drivers came to expect.

wide van would be shunned by customers, especially in cities. But aside from their intuition and the piles of feedback already

canvassed from users, Project Redcap personnel took one final acid test. Early one morning, they took a nondescript prototype down to the main fruit and vegetable market in Frankfurt, and showed it to the traders there. Their reaction was overwhelmingly positive; they declared that any van that was wider on the outside and wider on the inside had to be good for business.

American vans of the time, usually referred to as trucks, were a breed apart from cars, built to be immensely tough and mechanically straightforward as well as physically large. This pervaded the Redcap enterprise. So the 400E's more car-like independent front suspension was ditched in favour of a bomb-proof beam front axle. The standard engine would be a compact V4, with a four-speed all-synchromesh gearbox and recirculating ball steering.

◄◄ A very early Ford Transit Custom with optional sliding doors; it brought a new, American-style wide stance and styling to the market.

◄ Ford's compact V4 engines, which made their debut in the Corsair saloon car, found a natural home under the Transit's stumpy bonnet.

27

Britain, they used to say, is a nation of shopkeepers, and the Transit proved to be just the job for small businesses needing a beefy delivery vehicle.

The Transit rendered its opposition old bangers; users really valued its low and, in particular, wide cargo area.

28

The power unit would be mounted under a bonnet in front of the occupants, in what was called the forward-control position.

'Starting from scratch was a great advantage,' recalled Gordon Bird, one of the three leading Ford development engineering supervisors organising the team. 'It enabled us to take a fresh look at what our customers wanted, then meet their needs with a vehicle that was almost completely new from the ground up.

Ease of servicing was very important, because other vans tended to have important components tucked away in places which made even the simplest operations incredibly difficult. Mounting the engine in front of, rather than alongside, the van driver was a major improvement.' As a consequence, regular service items would be easily accessible, and especially electrical items like battery and fuses.

After about twenty engine-testing Redcap prototypes had been built, the first roadgoing examples sneaked out for secret road testing in January 1964. These Phase II and III experimental vehicles would undertake over 400,000 miles of hard driving to iron out faults and study durability. Gordon Bird looked after precisely 85,656 miles of sustained high-speed driving and – as there were no motorway speed limits at the time – the M2 in Kent made the perfect test route, as Ford lacked a suitable test track of its own. The vans were driven mostly at night to keep them from prying eyes, spending hour after hour cruising at 75mph. Police patrols did pull them over from time to time, but usually only to marvel at the fact that sometimes these vans were bombing along at up to 94mph.

The Swiss railways always run on time, partly aided by this track-going Transit introduced as a maintenance runabout in 1966.

The windscreen on the first-generation Transit was broad and deep, offering new standards of driver visibility; as there was a bonnet, wing mirrors could be fitted too.

◄ *Boxing legend Henry Cooper's Wembley greengrocery provided his day job, and a punchy Transit workhorse was essential in 1966 for the daily dawn run to Covent Garden.*

A demonstration of Transit strength at London Zoo, Regent's Park, in 1965; elephants must think humans are barmy.

At the same time, Redcap's brakes and cooling system were being rigorously perfected at the Motor Industry Research Association (MIRA) Centre's complex in Nuneaton, Warwickshire, where the wind tunnel was also utilised to improve stability. Test drivers took pre-production models to Belgium to spend spine-jarring days pounding the pavé cobbled streets there to discover how the suspension system held up under sustained punishment; others spent weeks in the French Alps, subjecting the brakes to long and steep gradients.

For easy starting, the new van's engine would have the unusual fitment – for a light commercial vehicle – of an alternator instead of a more basic dynamo. The winter of 1964/65 was a long and cold one in the UK, but Ford still insisted Redcap prototypes were taken to Finland, to the edge of the Arctic Circle, to ensure they could burst into life even at temperatures of -30°C.

At the other extreme, drivers were despatched with test vans down to the southern reaches of Europe. They took empty plastic jerry cans with them, intending to fill them with water when they reached Portugal so that hot-weather testing could be undertaken with heavy loads.

TRANSIT I: VITAL STATISTICS	
On sale:	1965–78
Wheelbase:	2692–2997mm
Length:	from 4885mm
Payload:	from 610kg
Engines:	1593–2994cc, V4 and in-line four-cylinder, and V6 six-cylinder, petrol; 1759–2360cc diesel

Did You Know?
To millions of children, the car star of 1968 movie classic *Chitty Chitty Bang Bang* has magical flying powers; in fact, the four cars built for filming used Ford Transit chassis fitted with Ford V6 engines.

Customs officers en route, however, suspected these were for an elaborate smuggling ruse, and 2,000 miles of valuable test distance was lost to protracted wrangles about whether the vans and their cargoes could actually cross the border!

And, as all of this was going on, back at Redcap's dual bases in Dagenham and Cologne, Ed Baumgartner was exercising his shuttle diplomacy, at one time apparently imprisoning an entire department of accountants in a room until they agreed on cost estimates for some vital components.

As to the look of the Transit, it was heavily Americanised, with bold horizontal styling lines pressed into the bodysides and prominent headlamps at the prow of each front wing. It looked butch and purposeful with a large curved windscreen and conventional, front-hinged doors featuring wind-down windows and quarterlights where most rivals had narrow and basic sliding windows.

On 8 October 1965, Redcap was unveiled to the public. It made a huge impact despite this also being the day when the Post Office Tower, the 620ft London landmark, was declared open. The new van was called the Ford Transit.

t was a new name to Britain, where Ford's old Thames sub-brand was being axed, but for the Germans, of course, the new vehicle was the Transit MkII. The Transit made history by becoming the first Ford created on a pan-European basis. In fact, the tentative project was deemed to have gone so well, despite a shaky start, that it led directly to the formation of Ford of Europe in 1967, an umbrella organisation

◄ *Ford Transits like this proved to be popular vehicles for the motorhome fraternity, and especially, for some reason, in Italy.*

that gradually integrated the company's European activities. The Escort of that year, which had been totally created in Britain, nonetheless also went into production in Germany, and then the Capri of 1969 became the first car developed the way the Transit had been.

Ford of Europe was headquartered in Brentwood, Essex, but the company had long considered the entire Eurozone for building new facilities. In 1962 it had picked Genk in Belgium as the site for a new assembly plant, and this was one of the two sources of the new Transit.

The other, the British one, was in Langley, Berkshire, where the earliest Transits came down the production line in what had been a former aircraft factory – indeed, once the home of the Hawker Hurricane. It was now the British source of Ford's commercial vehicles range, which in 1965 also included the Ford D Series light truck. Transit and D Series formed a two-pronged attack on Bedford, owned by Ford's arch-rival General Motors, whose CA van and TK lorry were market leaders, so the Transit was aiming for corporate glory as well as customer suitability.

Under the bonnet – that feature that helped define the Transit – Ford offered V4 petrol engines for the first time in a light commercial vehicle, in a choice of capacities of 1663 and 1996cc. The former was shared with the Ford Corsair and the latter with the Zephyr MkIV, and they were manufactured at Dagenham's 44-acre engine plant. With crossflow cylinder heads and bowl-shaped combustion chambers, they were efficient, gutsy and economical, while the combination of a big bore and

The D Series truck, launched in 1965 just like the Transit, helped Ford to swipe leadership of Britain's commercial vehicle market from Bedford.

39

The elongated nose marks this 1967 Transit milk float out as an early diesel, not an engine that endowed the vehicle with much bottle.

a short stroke gave the low piston speeds that promised excellent durability. 'We set out to produce a pair of compact engines giving power and flexibility right through the speed range,' explained Ford's chief power unit engineer, Alan Worters, at the time.

His team also planned a diesel V4, but too much work was required to refine it. Instead, the diesel option was provided by a 1759cc Perkins 4/99 engine, which gave miserly fuel economy but was decidedly gutless with just 41bhp on offer. It was restricted to the three lightest versions and the Transit Minibus only. Just a year after launch, Ford replaced it with the Perkins 4/108 that offered a slightly livelier 50bhp and was soon available across the whole Transit range. The diesel motors were longer than the V4 engines, and the extra bulk was accommodated behind an extended nose section that made them immediately distinctive.

From the word go, the range of Transit derivatives was huge, with 78 possible versions. The van itself could be had in both short- and long-wheelbase models. On top of this came various payload combinations that could tailor the vehicle to any business's exact projected use. The burliest offered a 3.5-tonne load-carrying ability, and this would definitely feature the twin sets of rear wheels – for traction consistency – that were another favourite feature for junior Transit spotters.

With the van's basic steel box as a starting point, Ford offered Transit minibuses from the start.

The picture says it all, of course; within five years the Transit's burgeoning success drove it to a new home, in Southampton.

◄ *On what basis this charming young lady was voted Miss Transit 1967 is not recorded, but she was not, perhaps, a mobile plumber.*

43

The company actually broke new ground in this sector by being the first to market 9-, 12- and 15-seater minibuses completely built in-house, with diesels capped at 11 seats so its wheezy engine could haul the thing up steep hills! In Germany, the 9-seater was marketed as a Kombi as a direct challenge to Volkswagen.

The most basic, short-wheelbase 1.7-litre Transit van cost £542 at the October 1965 launch, with the most expensive standard version being a long-wheelbase, 15-seater 2.0-litre minibus at £997.

◀ *Not every musician travelling by Transit was a gravel-voiced rock 'n' roller; this long-wheelbase minibus was used by Glyndebourne opera singers in 1968.*

Did You Know?
'Ford Transits are used in 95% of bank raids,' stated Metropolitan Police Commissioner Wallace Virgo in 1972. 'With a car's performance and space for 1.5 tons of loot, the Transit is proving the perfect getaway vehicle for villains . . . there are so many of them about that one could easily get lost in London traffic.'

A VERSATILE WORKHORSE TAKES MANY FORMS

In the past, the narrow Thames 400E had not been a popular choice as a base for bespoke bodywork. Now the Transit was changing all that, its broad track and straightforward, robust ladder frame chassis making it a natural starting point for all manner of specialist conversions. Via Ford's Special Vehicle Orders department, customers could peruse a thudding great *Transit Body Equipment Mounting Manual* which contained the details of the hundreds of bodywork options that had been granted factory approval.

Many of these bodies, constructed by specialist coachbuilders across the UK, turned the Transit into a dedicated load-carrier. Parcel van bodies made it ideal for stop-start city deliveries, while Luton vans (inspired by Bedfordshire's hat-making centre, these spacious vans featured a cargo area extending over the driver's cab for bulky but light loads) and other adaptations turned it into the tractor unit of a pint-sized articulated lorry. Transit pick-ups, dropsides and tipper trucks were soon commonplace on building sites, while flatbeds were pressed into service delivering things like coal, or given a horsebox rear end, or became milk floats and ice-cream vans.

The impact the Transit made on the British market was instant and extraordinary. Within a week of its launch, Ford had taken £3.6m-worth of Transit orders, with sales running ahead of expectations by 27%. Over in Germany, the Transit boosted Ford's light commercial vehicle market share – admittedly from a pretty lowly base – by 114%, and was starting to become a thorn in Volkswagen's side.

47

Children shared in the excitement too. Almost as soon as the real thing hit the showrooms, a Dinky Toys scale model of the Transit van was in toyshops, priced at 9s 11d and resplendent in the livery of the Kenwood kitchen appliance company.

But if there was one characteristic of Ford in the 1960s that set it apart from its competitors, it was a refusal to rest on its laurels. The company designed great products and, once they were on sale and had been well received, immediately set about making improvements. Not that much was awry with the Transit itself – just that ever more choices could be offered.

In 1967, then, came the option of Borg Warner automatic transmission on petrol-engined models, while high-compression V4 engines were also available from 1969. From that time on, Ford needed to be extra-alert to customers' desires because Bedford, with sales of its ageing CA decimated by the Transit, belatedly hit back with the all-new CF, a range of vans and chassis/cabs intended to match Ford at every level. The gloves were off . . .

The Transit went into action with the emergency services in 1966, when the first one configured as an ambulance left the Wilmslow workshops of Herbert Lomas Ltd under its 2-litre V4 power. The long-wheelbase chassis provided the stretcher-friendly low floor and Ford provided the low initial purchase cost that had attracted Worcester City local authority bean-counters.

In the same year, the Oxfordshire Constabulary became one of the first forces to adapt a Transit to a specific policing role. In this case, it was as a mobile control room

◄ Van-osaurus Rex? In 1973, this Transit flatbed took a 49ft-long plastic dinosaur from Kent to the Natural History Park in Scotland.

The first credible Transit rival arrived in 1969 with the release of Bedford's competent CF range, seen here in camper guise.

combining communications centre and emergency headquarters. A roof extension gave 20% more headroom so up to seven officers could work inside either incognito or, with the 35ft-long retractable antenna raised when using the 3-mile range radios, very much on the crime scene.

Other forces across the land ordered Transits, too. Many, such as Leicestershire Constabulary, had them kitted out as rapid-response units that could speed to accidents on motorways. Typically, these long-wheelbase vans were packed with first aid gear, cones, temporary signs and other equipment needed to clear wreckage, direct traffic and assist dazed survivors. They also featured the extended nose of the Transit diesel but, instead of the raucous clatter of the Perkins oil-burner, they emitted the throaty roar of a V6 engine. Ford's 3-litre Essex V6 was more usually found in the upmarket Zodiac or sportiest Capri and was available to special order in 'rapid response' Transits. With about 100bhp on tap, along with plenty of extra torque to give the Transit useful mid-range urge, it proved extremely popular in its special applications. One such engine in high Capri tune and fitted to a van with a front airdam for high-speed stability, was lapped at MIRA's test track at 108mph – an indecent speed for a mere delivery hack.

Dinky Toys updated its Kenwood Transit into a Police Accident Unit, complete with police livery and a cluster of tiny accessories, and created one of its best-selling models of the 1970s – now worth a fortune if it's in its original box and all the little cones and signs haven't been long ago sucked up a vacuum cleaner pipe. . . .

This is the Ford Transit Supervan, an eye-opening pre-race attraction at British circuits in the early 1970s. The bloke could be The Stig's grandpa, for all we know.

And nor was that the fastest of the early Transits. Essex-based engine tuning company Terry Drury Racing was tasked by Ford with turning a humble van into the ultimate hot-rod; a Supervan, no less. This they did by installing a 5-litre Ford USA V8 – exactly the same unit as found in the contemporary Gurney-Eagle racing car – in the loadbay of a standard short-wheelbase Tranny. Naturally, it would drive the rear wheels, although ultra-wide racing wheels and tyres were fitted front and back. It could reach 70mph in 9.7 seconds, cover a quarter-mile in 14.9 seconds, and was timed at 150mph. Supervan was a great crowd-pleaser, making its debut before 40,000 race fans at Thruxton at the Easter Monday meeting in 1971 – in demonstrations, cheers were always guaranteed when it lifted a front wheel under viciously hard acceleration.

It could seem, to the casual Transit admirer, that the van was synonymous with fun-and-games and popular culture. Writing in *New Society* magazine in 1970, Reyner Banham contributed an intriguing piece entitled 'In The Van Of Progress'. In it, he celebrated the Transit's rapid ascension to popular culture icon, as the vehicle of choice for performers as they toured the music venues of Britain and Europe. Rock and roll stars as diverse as Elton John, the Small Faces and Brian Poole & The Tremeloes all pounded the tarmac night after night rattling around in the back of Transits, no doubt accompanied by plenty of instruments and, ahem, refreshments to keep them going through the small hours. 'That van,' wrote Banham, 'is as much part of The Life as roadies and groupies and (picking my words carefully) one-night stands.'

If you can remember the 1960s, as they say, then you weren't there.

The trusty Transit underwent one of the most important changes in its life so far in 1972. Ford engineers were acutely aware that the diesel engines used in the range, bought in from Peterborough-based supplier Perkins, endowed the vehicle with notably lacklustre performance, despite making it very thrifty. So they set about designing their own – from scratch. The results were revealed on 5 January when the 2.4-litre York diesel engine was announced.

Ford motors had a reputation for eager performance, and the York was no exception. The four-cylinder engine produced a decent 62bhp at 3600rpm, which made it 25% more powerful than the old Perkins 4/108 lump as well as generating 25% more torque. This made any Transit fitted with it significantly more responsive, flexible and generally urgent-feeling in every department.

Recognising the long-term needs of Transit operators, Ford began working on the York in 1967. Prototypes were being bench-tested within a year, followed by four years of punishing real-life tests; 150 engines ran for 50,000 hours, which included spells of continuous running for 1,000 hours at full load, or relentless stopping-and-starting to simulate the daily grind of a diesel Transit doing hectic city deliveries.

From a driver's viewpoint – indeed, to the benefit of everybody within earshot of a York engine – the fitting of a toothed-belt drive for the camshaft and injection pump, instead of chains or gears, made the engine much less clattery. Ford sunk £11.5m in the development of the York, and its manufacture at Dagenham laid the cornerstone for what is, today, Ford's global centre of diesel engine manufacture

at the Essex plant. York's introduction, and the imitators it inspired, had an enormous influence on the decisions van buyers made about their vehicles; petrol engines became marginalised and diesel engines took over as the default choice.

That said, in 1975, the petrol engines available in the Transit underwent a major change too. The old 1.7-litre V4 was dropped and in came a 1.6-litre in-line, four-cylinder overhead-valve engine. The overhead-camshaft, short-stroke, crossflow-head design was first used in the Cortina in 1967, and added renewed zest to the smallest-engined Transit. Consequently, front-wheel disc brakes were also standardised in 1976. A year later, Ford's own, French-built automatic transmission replaced the Borg Warner item in the Transit.

Production of the Transit topped the 1 million mark on 15 September 1976, almost exactly 10 years after its introduction. It was a minibus immediately shipped to its buyer in Nigeria. Some 420,000 of them had been assembled in Belgium and the 580,000 balance in the UK. Ford had a habit in this period of outgrowing its factory space. Just as the commercial vehicles had been shifted from Dagenham to Langley, Berkshire, now the rip-roaring success of the Transit, and also the swelling demand for the D Series lorry, meant a new home had been sought for the van range alone.

Ever since 1953, the bodywork for Ford's bigger vans and the cabs for its lorries had been built at a former aircraft components plant at Swaythling, Southampton. The 630,000sq ft factory opened in 1939 and where once parts for Spitfire aircraft were

We worried that it might be sexist to include this image of Penthouse Racing's Transit support van, but then we thought you'd appreciate a good view of the 1975 grille design, so kept it in.

This luxurious 1976 camper interpretation of the Transit is the Travelhome, fitted with central heating and double-glazing. Must have been a fuel-hungry way to avoid hotel bills.

produced, from 1965 bodies for the Transit – another heroic icon of British engineering – were manufactured and then transported to Langley for assembly. This complicated arrangement was ended in 1972 when Ford spent £5m on turning Southampton into the Transit's dedicated British home, centring manufacture and assembly on the Swaythling site. The first complete van to be built there was presented to the Mayor of Southampton who donated it to a local youth charity, and henceforth the Transit has been the most significant symbol of the coastal city's local manufacturing economy.

In 1978, a completely revamped Transit arrived. It wasn't quite a full 'MkII' because the basic structure and shape remained identical, but the revisions were extensive.

The most obvious change was a redesigned frontage that was more aerodynamic and now gave the same look to all models no matter what engine was behind the neat, black plastic slatted grille and square headlights. Much more important to everyday Transit drivers was a redesigned cabin and a refined suspension that reduced the impact of the day's knocks and jolts.

All traces of the old V4 engine range were now eradicated. All petrol engines were now overhead-camshaft units, in 1.6- and 2.0-litre forms, similar to those in the best-selling Cortina saloon. They were more powerful, offered more torque and, in the case of the 1.6, boosted fuel economy by 25%. Even the York came in for some attention, gaining a glowplug system to make starting easy even on the iciest mornings when diesels are not easily awoken from their slumber.

◀◀ *Muhammad Ali causes a sensation in 1977 during the handover of a Transit ambulance for disabled children by the Variety Club of Great Britain.*

◀ *In 1977 PepsiCo created this mobile British advertisement for its fizzy drinks on the basis of a short-wheelbase Transit.*

➤ An all-new nose for the Transit denoted the second-generation model in 1978, in this case a short-wheelbase crew bus for the Central Electricity Generating Board.

➤➤ In 1978 Radio Luxembourg – no doubt inspired by the Radio 1 Roadshow – decided to take its own show around Europe, using this Transit van.

▶ Quite a few Transits have been customised over the years, but few as radically as this space-age six-wheeler in 1979.

So what of the Transit's rivals in the late 1970s? Throughout the entire decade, General Motors' Bedford CF was probably its closest and most consistent sparring partner, although it never once outsold the Transit. Meanwhile, it took Austin Morris until 1974 to turn the also-ran J4 into the Sherpa. By British Leyland's crummy standards, it was a trouble-free product, and many liked its city-friendly narrow track, but the bite that the Sherpa took out of Ford's sales was never threateningly large. Chrysler UK's Commer/Dodge Spacevan was a feeble 1960s relic. Imports from France, Italy and Spain were negligible at the time, with exported Transits far more likely to be heading in the opposite direction. Volkswagen's rear-engined Transporter vans were credible alternatives to the smallest Transits, as was the Toyota Hi-Ace that was making a semi-regular appearance on Britain's roads, but relied on the old-fashioned forward-control configuration that the Transit had helped to render so unpopular. And neither could be so easily custom-designed for specific tasks.

TRANSIT II: VITAL STATISTICS	
On sale:	1978–86
Wheelbase:	2692–3000mm
Length:	from 4997mm
Payload:	from 610kg
Engines:	1593–2994cc, in-line four-cylinder, and V6 six-cylinder, petrol; 2360–2496cc diesel

One of the few Transit IIs that could be described as a real stinker – note the optionally available, top-hinged tailgate.

◄ It's 1980 and a group of Brownies contemplate a hot, sticky journey home from camp in this Transit II long-wheelbase minibus.

67

Transits have long been favourites with the construction industry; this heavy-duty long-wheelbase van is caught on-site in 1980.

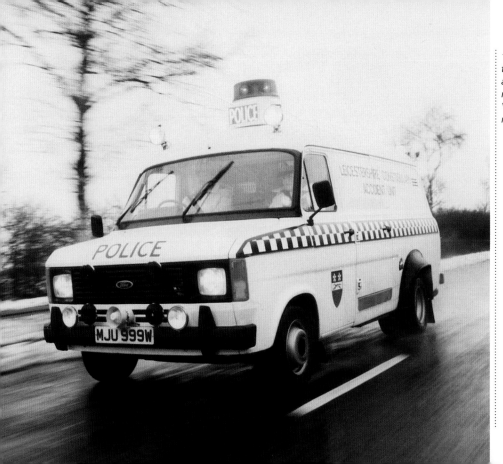

◀ *Transits supplied to police forces and ambulance fleets routinely used powerful V6 engines for 'rapid responses'.*

◄◄ *Gung-ho stuntman Steve Matthews jumped fifteen cars in this old Transit I van in 1985 to raise money for a cancer charity; note the high-quality door and bonnet locks. . . .*

◄ *This is the 174mph Supervan II built to amuse racing fans, really a rebodied C100 endurance racer with a V8 Cosworth engine . . . in the back.*

The Transit entered the 1980s as dominant as ever. As such an honest, straightforward product, there wasn't much mystery to its appeal and market success, but it was strange that other manufacturers seemed reluctant to take the Transit on directly. Indeed, the Bedford CF would peter out in the late 1980s, replaced in the GM range by the Midi, a licence-built version of a forward-control Isuzu design that ruled Bedford out for many customers.

The next Transit landmark broke new ground technically. In 1984 a new DI diesel engine was unveiled as a successor to the venerable York unit. A 2.5-litre development of the basic York unit, it was the world's first small, non-turbo diesel automotive engine with direct fuel injection. Rigorously tested over 110,000 hours of lab time and 500,000 miles on the road, its 25% reduction in fuel thirst, not to mention its livelier performance from 68bhp and useful extra torque, resulted in it winning a Motor Industry Design Award from the Design Council in 1985. It also meant that the glowplug quick fix in the ignition system could be dropped. It became an option on Transits during 1984, and soon consigned the York, its own glory intact, to history. Those '84 Transits were that bit sleeker too, with a new front airdam. In 1985, just such a model became the 2-millionth Transit to roll off the production line – in this case, at Southampton.

On 9 January 1986, a brand new Ford Transit greeted an expectant world. A new page was being turned on what had become a truly legendary vehicle – one that had been the best-selling light commercial vehicle in Britain for every one of its 20 years on sale so far. Owing to the sustained success of its Transit, Ford had had to think long and hard about its replacement. The Transit alone survived the company's decision to flog off its trucks business, and its Langley factory, to IVECO in 1986. It was easy to see why. In 1978, Ford could boast that it held 20% of the entire British commercial vehicle market; but almost two out of every three vans and trucks it sold were Transits – everything else was a sideshow. No wonder the company was prepared to spend £400m on creating the new one, of which £100m would be lavished on the plants in Southampton and Genk so they could make a seamless manufacturing transition.

In the end, then, and despite its radical new appearance, the 'all-new' vehicle was

◀ The 2.5-litre DI was the world's first small automotive engine with direct fuel-injection, and first appeared in the Transit II in 1984.

TRANSIT III: VITAL STATISTICS

On sale: 1986–91

Wheelbase: 2815–2835mm

Length: from 4632mm

Payload: from 833kg

Engines: 1593–2994cc, in-line four-cylinder, and V6 six-cylinder, petrol; 2496cc diesel

in fact a thorough but careful evolution of everything buyers had come to expect of the Transit. Almost every component was reshaped, redesigned or refined, yet the existing underpan and chassis were retained, as were the 1.6- and 2.0-litre petrol engines and the just-launched 2.5DI diesel.

These power units, obviously, were still housed ahead of the driver in the 'normal-control' position. However, in place of a protruding bonnet, the cab now featured what stylists at Ford had termed a 'fast front', with a steeply raked bonnet line and windscreen forming one, wind-cheating plane from the headlights to the top of the screen. It gave the new van an impressive coefficient of drag – the measure of how aerodynamic it was – of 0.37, as well as giving, thanks to a deep screen/side

◀ Italy's Ghia design studio, owned by Ford, was better known for creating sleek concept cars in 1986, when it came up with this one-off Transit show van, the Chasseur, featuring stylish side glazing treatment.

◀◀ It was all change in 1985 for the radical-looking Transit III; this one is a German-market crew cab dropside pick-up.

Inside the cab was a totally new dashboard and facia clearly inspired by those found in Ford passenger cars like the Sierra and Scorpio, as part of a more ergonomic interior. Researchers had spent hundreds of hours riding shotgun with a wide spectrum of Transit drivers as the new model (codenamed VE6 by Ford insiders) took shape, so most of the improvements were geared to easier everyday use. This programme led to the fitment of a new five-speed manual gearbox on all but the lowly 1.6-litre petrol models.

It also strongly influenced the decision to split the Transit into light- and heavy-duty versions. The big-payload toughies retained the beam front axle with their old-fashioned but super-strong leaf springs, along with the ponderous but rock-solid recirculating ball steering.

▲ Inside the 1986 Ghia Chasseur was a super-opulent mobile office-cum-boardroom, whose on-board electronic goodies included a whopping great 'mobile' phone.

window line, vastly better driver visibility. To the outside world, it looked as if the Transit had been strongly influenced by the most adventurous car of the era, the Renault Espace, credited as one of the first multi-passenger vehicles (MPVs).

▲ London's Capital Radio drivers circled the newly-completed M25 for seven continuous days and nights in 1986 in this special Transit.

▲ Ford is renowned for helping film-makers create on-screen action, in this case with a Transit in the Michael Caine thriller The Fourth Protocol in 1987.

◄ Transit III proved as versatile as ever – the separate-chassis model here serving as the basis for a very compact refuse truck.

77

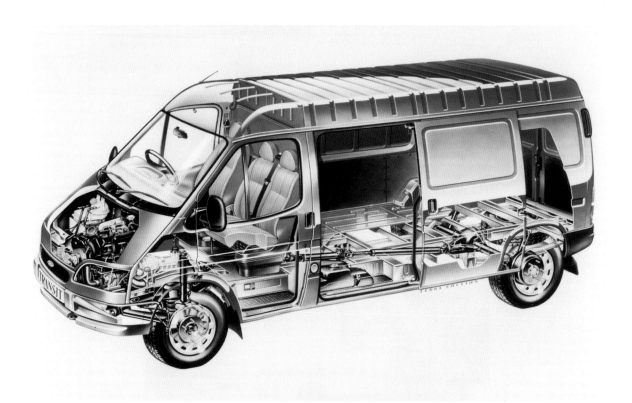

◀◀ *The fourth-generation Transit series of 1991 revolved around an engineering rethink to boost safety, increase space and reduce operator costs.*

◀ *The third incarnation of Supervan arrived in 1995, boasting 650bhp of Cosworth power bellowing all the way up to 13,000rpm.*

MASON'S YARD

◄◄ *Ford's RS200 was a star of the short-lived Group B, a rally class banned for being dangerously fast. Naturally, the company built the car a special tender, based on the Transit III.*

◄ *Transit IV long-wheelbase models had a vastly longer wheelbase so twin sets of rear wheels could be done away with; this is a high-top van edition.*

At the back they sported the twin pairs of rear wheels familiar from Transits past. But for the lighter models, and especially the vans that would be driven by company employees or individuals more used to cars than trucks, there was independent front suspension by a version of MacPherson strut together with rack-and-pinion steering, all of which made the Transit easier to handle and much more nimble-feeling.

That Ford had got the new range spot-on was clear from sales. Production doubled by 1989, with 78,500 rolling out of Southampton that year against a mere 38,900 of the previous model in 1985. This pattern was repeated in Genk. The new Transit was, suddenly, on every street in Britain.

The vehicles continued to sell like hot cakes. And the first major improvement didn't come along until 1988, when a worked-over diesel engine was introduced, cutting exhaust emissions in line with prevailing laws but also upping power very slightly to 70bhp.

'VE6' fitted the bill for Transit operators to a tee, and Ford bided its time when it came to finessing the successful formula. In 1992, however, a comprehensive raft of changes turned it into the 'VE64'. It represented a determination, thanks to a £300m investment, to improve the Transit's safety and user practicality.

Behind the cab, a redesigned underfloor section replaced the unit that had been largely unchanged since the Transit's 1965 debut. There were two, equally important reasons for this. Firstly, it was to beef up the structure so that the wheelbase of the long-wheelbase model could be extended

> *Transits continued to be a popular choice for motorhome conversions, this beauty based on a MkIV being the Herald Aragon. Two kids and a baby in a camper van for a week? Hmm. . . .*

> *There was an obscenely large-wheeled pick-up in the US known as 'Big Foot' that inspired this rock-hopping Transit IV in 1994; the axles are from a US military vehicle, the transmission from a London bus.*

by a massive 21.6in, or 55cm. This meant it could handle its tasks without twin sets of rear wheels at the back, making the van cheaper to run (less tyres to replace!) and, crucially, allow less intrusion of the wheelarches into the load area – it would increase its width by a substantial 14.4in/36.5cm.

Secondly, the Transit had to meet modern requirements for surviving a 30mph crash. The new structure was designed to handle such an impact, along with reinforcements to the cab structure, seats and seatbelt mountings to protect occupants in a shunt. From now on, too, all Transits would have independent front suspension systems, eliminating the truck-like front beam axle option and making every new Transit easier to drive.

But that was not all: there was a six-year anti-perforation rust warranty to please fleet owners, while drivers enjoyed the reassurance of standard anti-lock braking with ventilated disc brakes upfront. The big news engine-wise was the availability of a 2.5DI turbodiesel. For long-distance driving this offered 100bhp, a 42% power boost, along with a 52% increase in torque that added real mid-range flexibility for overtaking.

This new Transit was simply better all round, but just to top it off there was a styling update in September 1994 with the 'VE83' Transit. Ford's friendly-looking oval grille shape now adorned the Transit's sloping nose but, in case people thought it was mere window-dressing, the revised range included three new features.

TRANSIT IV: VITAL STATISTICS	
On sale:	1991–4
Wheelbase:	3020–3570mm
Length:	from 4632mm
Payload:	from 795kg
Engines:	1593–2933cc, in-line four-cylinder, and V6 six-cylinder, petrol; 2496cc diesel

◀ *Some clever hydraulics went into creating this six-wheeled 'folding' Transit recovery vehicle.*

For those few Transit buyers who opted for petrol power, an all-new Ford twin overhead-camshaft 2-litre engine was now fitted – the sort of power unit more usually associated, at that time, with sports cars. As there was a sparkling 114bhp of power coming out of this sophisticated, fuel-injected power unit, Ford could finally delete the V6 engine that had been available to special order, and considerable complexity in terms of fitting, in emergency services versions of older Transits.

◄◄ *Three-point seatbelts as standard for every seat was an important safety upgrade on the MkV.*

◄ *All Transits come filled with free air in the back as standard, apart from this RAC hot-air balloon Transit, where it has to be paid for.*

Of far more importance to the bulk of Transit buyers, however, was the optional fitment of front airbags and standard three-point seatbelts across all three seats in the cab. There was a new facia, better heating and ventilation, and air-conditioning was now an option.

TRANSIT V: VITAL STATISTICS

On sale:	1994–2000
Wheelbase:	2835–3570mm
Length:	from 4632mm
Payload:	from 795kg
Engines:	1998cc, petrol; 2496cc, diesel

🔺 *The first Transit to be built in China was completed in 1997, where locally-sourced Isuzu or Mitsubishi engines were fitted.*

The newly-evolved Transit went global. The vans had long been assembled in Turkey, beginning with kits of parts sent from Western Europe but slowly changing to include a higher percentage of locally-made components, and the VE83 built on its success there with 9,000 made in 1995 and 25,700 the following year. Other assembly operations popped up in Poland and Portugal, but the Transit also went into Chinese production in 1997 in partnership with the Jiangling Motor Corporation near Shanghai, where various locally produced Isuzu and Mitsubishi engines and other parts were adapted to fit the Transit structure.

◄◄ This line-up of Transit V chassis variants amply demonstrates how just about any type of light commercial vehicle can be built on their strong steel frames.

◄ A Transit V dropside pick-up in its natural habitat in 1995 – it can be accessed by a forklift, or a brickie, on three sides.

91

Small tipper trucks frequently use the Transit as a basis, with the tipper section supplied by several outside body makers.

In the late 1990s, the Transit was a familiar sight on TV in Britain, thanks to the simple but effective 'Backbone of Britain' advertising campaign. It showed trusty Transits serving the country's everyday delivery needs in dramatic fashion. However, despite being largely untroubled by competition from the 1960s to the 1980s, the 1990s were very different, with competent alternatives to the Transit seemingly everywhere. The Franco-Italian Fiat Ducato/Peugeot Boxer/Citroën Relay, together with the Renault Trafic, was one source of rivalry, a phalanx of Japanese models another. But the really significant challenges hailed from Germany.

Volkswagen's Transporter, already sitting astride a phenomenal reputation, entered its fourth generation in 1990 with a shock change in direction: it was now front-engined and front-wheel, drive, ushering in a new era of ever more car-like driveability. Previously a threat to the smaller and lighter Transits, there was now also a long-wheelbase/high-payload model.

 *Tens of thousands of Transit vans go through this procedure each day in Britain, usually as their drivers gulp down tea and bacon sandwiches before hitting the road.*

In 1990, Volkswagen's Transporter switched to front-wheel drive, and began to alter drivers' expectations of light vans.

Meanwhile – and as hinted at in the introduction to this book – the Transit was assailed at the medium to heavy end of the payload spectrum by the Mercedes-Benz Sprinter, introduced in 1995.

It was almost as if Merc had asked customers what they wanted in a van and they'd replied, en masse, that they desired a Ford Transit but a Ford Transit made by Mercedes-Benz. The Sprinter's visual

BT, and its predecessor British Telecom, has long run one of the largest Transit fleets in the country – remember BT's 'piper' logo introduced to such derision in 1991?

For Mercedes-Benz, the dream was to snatch a big chunk of Transit sales with its curiously similar Sprinter in 1995, and it largely hit the target.

resemblance to the Transit was uncanny. To reinforce Mercedes' ambition to chase van buyers, there was a new small Vito van, too.

Not only that, but Merc thrust its Sprinter into the US market – the one major territory where the Transit had always been absent.

THE BIG SPLIT MAKES HISTORY, WITH A LITTLE HELP FROM AMERICA

Consequently, in 1995, work began in earnest on the Ford van that would catapult the Transit into the twenty-first century and all the challenges that it would face.

The trouble was – literally – where to start. With no complete European commercial vehicles division any longer, a brand new Transit would require an engineering team built from scratch in an environment heavily focused on cars. Yet, as the Transit was so profitable for Ford, there could be no half measures when it came to getting its successor bang-on.

Hence, after much debate, wrangling and persuasion within the multinational Ford company, it was decided to engineer the new Transit in the USA where the company had a thriving truck operation. Up to 40 British staff moved to Detroit to work with over 500 other designers and engineers using the very latest computer-aided design software. As if that wasn't a radical enough move, there was a long and ongoing thought process centring on what kind of vehicle the new Transit ought to be.

The Transit was intrinsic to the growth of so-called 'home shopping' in Britain, even before the internet age clicked into life; this long-wheelbase Transit is doing its doorstep rounds in 1997.

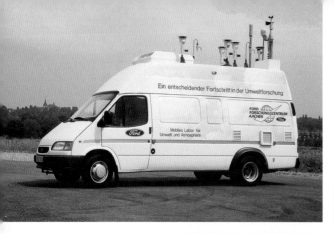

▲ A Transit V kitted out as a mobile air quality laboratory, with four rear wheels necessary to haul it from one smog spot to the next.

➤ Ford unveiled this design exercise in 1998 to soften customers up for the Transit design revolution that lay ahead.

▲ The Transit VI of 2000 represented the first totally and utterly new Transit since Ford launched the first one in 1965.

➤ The bare bones of a Transit VI minibus come together amid the robotic clatter and whirr of the Southampton bodyshop in 2005.

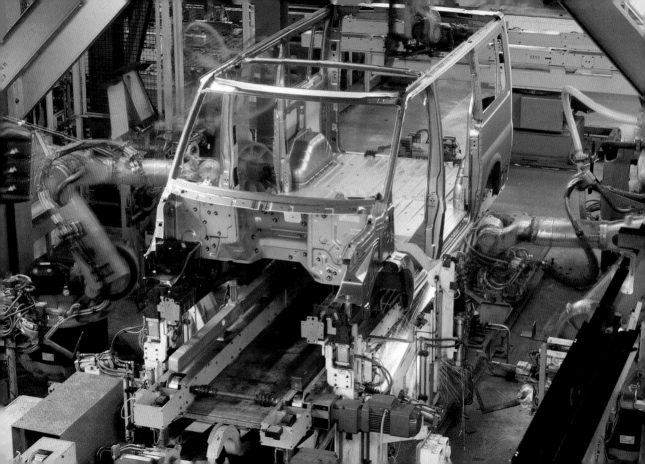

Front-wheel drive arrived for the Transit in 2000, helping to make the driving experience less of an ordeal for drivers accustomed to modern cars.

On the one hand were the traditionalists in Europe, who were well aware that the dependable reputation of the van range hinged on the simplicity of its front-engined, rear-drive layout; even more conservative, in many ways, were their new US colleagues, to whom US trucks were heavy, robust and resolutely old-school in their engineering. On the other, though, were the modernisers and visionaries, who could see not only the pleasant, modern driving characteristics of front-wheel drive but also the significant packaging benefit of positioning the whole drivetrain at the front end, freeing up cargo space at the other.

For a time, it looked like two entirely separate vans might be developed, just as Mercedes-Benz offered the compact Vito and larger Sprinter. But eventually, Ford went for the most radical option of all: one basic piece of vehicle architecture in which either front- or rear-wheel drive could be offered. It was something that had never before been tried. Transatlantic work continued apace, and in March 2000 the results were ready to be revealed.

There were two codenames this time around, the rear-drive V184 and front-

◄ *The soft contours of the dashboard and minor controls design in the MkVI Transit helped create a more soothing cabin ambience from which to shout 'Oi, ΣΔϖ%*œ, are you blind or what?'*

⌃ The availability of both front- and rear-wheel drive in the MkVI Transit naturally facilitated four-wheel drive versions, such as this commodious and capable long-wheelbase minibus.

drive V185. From the outside, it was hard to tell which was which, although the return of twin rear wheels on the heaviest payload V184 range was one obvious clue. The achievement was incredible: 95% of the basic structure was identical on both versions, even though the rear-drive one used engines mounted in-line with the transmission and the front-drive one featured a transversely-mounted engine

⌃ Standard European and British building materials pallets were carefully studied and accommodated, even though MkVI design largely took place in the USA.

across the front of the vehicle. A major, yet little appreciated, hurdle had been overcome by the use of a universal rack in the rack-and-pinion steering that worked for both configurations. There was an

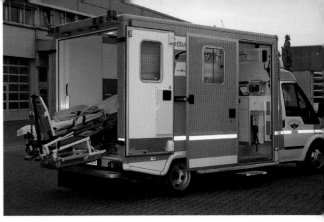

△ *The basic platforms offered by the Transit in its many variations act as the foundation for all sorts of eventual vehicles.*

△ *This specialised, fully equipped ambulance, in service in the city of Cologne, shows what can be built on the longest-wheelbase Transit.*

undeniable sense of theatre when Ford demonstrated, to watching media in 2000, a component swap in which a rear-drive Transit was converted to a front-drive one in just 20 minutes!

It was all change in the engines department. They were all four-cylinder units new to the Transit: the petrol engine was a 2.3-litre, 16-valve double-overhead camshaft unit and was always expected to sell in small numbers. It could now be had only in the rear-drive Transit, in which the diesel option was now a Ford Duratorq 2.4-litre 16-valve in states of tune from 75 to 137bhp.

This rear-wheel drive Transit has what's known as a demountable body, in this case a pen for collecting and transporting waste.

In the front-drive Transit only came a smaller 2.0-litre Duratorq in 75 to 125bhp form. They all came with five-speed manual gearboxes, and the conventional auto option was now replaced by a clutch-less Durashift on rear-drive Transits only.

American Dave Grandinett was the chief programme engineer on the all-new Transit. He'd been responsible for front-drive prototypes hitting the road a full three-and-a-half years before it went on sale, to allow plenty of time to hone every aspect. They ended up covering almost 5 million real-time miles of driving and over 1.8 million miles of 'severe condition' simulated tests, while the bodywork was subjected to durability trials in vats of the saltiest water Ford could concoct.

'Front-drive and rear-drive Transit have their own personalities . . . they're very different-feeling vehicles in the way they project themselves, what they feel like to drive,' he commented at the time of the launch. 'A front-drive Transit feels like a sport truck. It seems to say "throw me around. Play with me. I'll carry the load, but let's have some fun doing it".'

Although a rarity, it is possible to turn a Transit into a miniature articulated truck, where the vehicle acts as the tractor unit. Special tuition for drivers of this kettle of fish, one hopes, is always given.

For loads that are light but bulky, then a Transit-based Luton van's what's needed; this one has moulded side panels for better aerodynamics. And would be ideal to cram full of hats.

Cavernous load space, and lots of it, inside a high-roof Transit VI van.

The sculptural new cab was fully redesigned, with notably deep glass at front and sides. The bonnet could be locked, a novel and useful tool in industry's never-ending fight against pilferers and thieves. The interior was completely new, with an emphasis on providing places everywhere for the paraphernalia of the typical tradesmen whose daily activities Ford researchers had examined all over again; there were cupholders and even a mobile phone cradle. And while the steering wheel was more horizontal than ever, and so more car-like, the commanding driving position that Transit drivers had come to expect was undiminished.

▶ The smaller, front-wheel drive Transits make ideal business tools for the self-employed tradesman, craftsman or artisan.

TRANSIT VI: VITAL STATISTICS	
On sale:	2000–6
Wheelbase:	2933–3750mm
Length:	from 4834mm
Payload:	from 713kg
Engines:	2295cc, petrol; 1998–2402cc, diesel

New urethane bumpers were able to absorb energy and protect the suspension from impact damage.

On sale first were the rear-drive Transits, followed six months later in September 2000 by the front-drives. Factories in Southampton, Genk and Kocaeli, Turkey, had been re-equipped to build the hugely complex new range – £200m had been lavished on Southampton alone. Most other assembly plants were closed down and, indeed, Genk would lose the Transit altogether in 2004 (the Belgians would then concentrate on the Ford Mondeo) so that all European Transits would henceforth hail from the UK or Turkey. The Transit catalogue included, in vans alone, a choice of three wheelbases, three body cube heights and four load lengths, all designed to accommodate standard-sized British and European builders' material packs and pallets. The front-drive vans could boast some of the lowest cargo floors in their class, which sometimes meant a forklift was no longer needed to load and unload. There was a commensurate range of minibuses, boosted in 2002 by the addition of high-capacity 17-seaters.

Did You Know?
Probably Britain's most unusual Transit fleet were the vehicles carrying workers – and dynamite – around the labyrinthine tunnels of ICI's Cheshire salt mines. By 1985, there were 16 of them, all of which had had to be cut in two to get them down the mine's lift shaft and then reassembled once 500ft underground.

A BRITISH INSTITUTION THAT KEEPS ON DELIVERING

The 5-millionth Ford Transit was built at Southampton on 18 July 2005, as Ford released one of its famous statistical boasts: enough Transits had now been built to cover the entire length of the UK 15 times bumper to bumper. Robin Trowbridge, a Southampton employee who had built the vehicles for 32 years, had the honour of driving it off a production line now capable of churning out 375 examples daily. The white minibus was presented to cricketer Mike Gatting on behalf of the youth special needs charity The Lord's Taverners.

After the sad news that the MG Rover plant at Longbridge, Birmingham, was to shut down in 2005, the Transit offered some motor industry cheer. It was a wholly British product, with engines coming from Dagenham and transmissions from Halewood to Southampton to be installed in the finished vehicles. Some of the 1,441 employees there starred, alongside real actors, in a TV commercial filmed at the plant in 2005 to celebrate the Transit's 40th birthday. In 2004, a record number – 70,674 units – had been manufactured, with half going for export.

The venerable frontage of the Southampton plant where all British-made Transits have hailed from since 1972; it was once an aircraft factory, turning out Spitfire parts.

The surface of a just-painted Transit is inspected for quality as yet another van shell heads towards the Southampton assembly line.

The TDCi engine that powers the vast majority of new Transits is renowned for its reliability and sterling performance.

The seventh-generation Transit took its bow in 2006 with a bold new frontal appearance; here, a double-cab in-van edition for the maintenance and the human resources departments to argue over.

◄ *After 40 years on sale, this Transit inches along the production line at Southampton on its way to making history.*

Red and white van man: builder Neil Cottam and his 1966 Transit flatbed, which in 2005 was declared the oldest working Transit in Britain.

Ford isn't an organisation given easily to retrospection, but it is savvy to the heritage of its many famous products. Public affection matters to Ford, and the Transit means a lot to the British.

In February 2005, the company set out to find the oldest Ford Transit still in everyday use, and its search eventually turned up Neil Cottam in Preston, Lancashire.

He was still using a 1966 25cwt twin rear-wheel flatbed pick-up for his job in the building trade. 'It still has its Perkins 4/108 engine. It may not be a museum exhibit but it's fully drivable,' he said about the 46,000-mile truck. 'It's been on the road for 39 years. and all of that with just 50 horsepower.' Neil's daily workhorse, amusingly, was a Transit 'just' 40 years old. He was exactly the sort of chap catered for by the first Ford Transit Owners' Club,

also founded in 2005. It was the idea of Peter Lee, owner of both the oldest known surviving Transit (a van once owned by electrical giant GEC) and a 20,000-strong collection of van models. Within two years, his fan club had 600 members.

▲ *The Transit facia is designed with ergonomics foremost; note the gearlever that now sprouts from the dashboard instead of from the floor.*

◄▲ *Optional four-wheel drive turns the Transit into a vehicle that can make light of slippery conditions, for work or leisure.*

◄ *A Transit VII standard van is big enough for most, but larger box vans are available, with a hydraulic tail-lift to cut out the lifting aggro.*

▲ *Just what they like in Southampton – a nice big order for 56 identical Transits that, in AA livery, will soon be ferrying replacement windscreens to stricken member drivers.*

► *Transits are as happy towing trailers as they are hauling their own loads; this is a mobile satellite dish for a Belgian TV company out filming L'Apprentice, or something. . . .*

The standard cab interior is a million miles from the sparse and tinny 1965 original – it positively cossets the driver and his two mates.

A dash-top storage box on the MkVII keeps lunch cool, even if many White Van Men are unfamiliar with fresh fruit and cereal bars!

A very welcome feature for drivers slogging through a hot shift in today's Transit is this under-dash nacelle that can hold a 2-litre bottle of liquid refreshment.

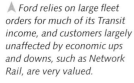 Ford relies on large fleet orders for much of its Transit income, and customers largely unaffected by economic ups and downs, such as Network Rail, are very valued.

This wacky Transit XXL 'limousine' was built, as a one-off, to mark the Transit's 40th birthday in 2005.

The tipper body on the back of this Transit can tilt in three directions, making it exceptionally handy in tight working conditions.

◀◀ *Another sought-after configuration on the current MkVII Transit is this one, with lockable storage cupboards in the centre and a short-length tipper at the back.*

◀ *The biggest standard passenger-carrying Transit today is this 17-seater minibus, with rear-wheel drive.*

Transit minibuses like this 15-seater are a common sight all over the UK because they offer practical people-carrying with a frugal fuel thirst.

A stylistic MkVII (V347 for FWD and V348 for RWD) revamp in 2006 saw the previously sleek Transit MkVI receive a brassy frontal makeover, with a much more prominent and upright grille and bolder headlights. The diesel engine in the front-wheel drive models increased in capacity to 2.2-litre, and all diesel engines now featured high-pressure common-rail technology.

The idea of a sporty delivery van is, to some, a contradiction in terms, but the SportVan certainly looks the business with its stripes, fancy paintwork and alloy wheels.

During the last five years, the Transit's fortunes have ridden the rollercoaster endured by the wider British economy. In 2009, 500 staff were laid off at Southampton as demand plummeted, after the workforce there had already endured shift cuts and a 20-day shutdown. Van sales always take a beating in recessions; from selling over 57,214 Transits in Britain in 2003, only 36,760 found buyers in 2009, although this figure rose to 46,300 in 2010. Volatile territory, then. And there is even more pressure on Ford workers in Britain from their productive Turkish counterparts, where in 2000 the new Kocaeli plant became the global 'lead' factory for Transit production, as well as later introducing the smaller Ford van branded as the Transit Connect.

No gloomy outlook could take the shine off the Transit's 45th birthday celebrations in October 2010. Simultaneously, Ford could boast that the 6-millionth example had been built at one of its 22 locations, of which China was now an important constituent.

◀ Whitby Morrison of Crewe are Britain's top ice cream van makers, and naturally offer a Transit-based model on which the entire rear section is custom-made.

TRANSIT VII: VITAL STATISTICS

On sale:	2006–
Wheelbase:	2933–3750mm
Length:	from 4863mm
Payload:	from 948kg
Engines:	2261cc, petrol; 2198–2402cc, diesel

▶ The Transit Connect is the big van's baby brother, and is made in Turkey. However, all the duo shares is that famous brand name.

▶▶ The lustrous blue paint and silver highlights of the special edition Transit Sapphire, built to celebrate the van's 45th birthday in 2010.

▶ *The special edition Transit Sapphire is a front-wheel drive van that's very pleasant to drive, even on long, boring motorway trips with not many opportunities to tailgate.*

▶▶ *The 2010 Tribute motorhome was among the first to utilise the lightweight, specially designed Transit camper chassis.*

The Jumbo rear-wheel drive Transit VII offers the ultimate in cargo space on a factory-built, steel-panelled van. Bigger than some people's houses, that.

Ford responded to the situation in the best way it knows: with new products. While there was a limited edition ink-blue-and-silver Sapphire van to mark the birthday milestone, rather more significant was the introduction of a lightweight chassis for motorhome conversions, available in three wheelbase lengths. It featured reduced height and weight for extra payload and rather better fuel economy, and could be ordered with an extra-wide rear axle to maximise the interior accommodation. Swivelling 'captain's' front seats were factory-fitted. The Transit already had a long history as a popular base for campers; in Italy, until 1973, the more traditional Volkswagen Transporter didn't get a look-in, as 8,000 Transits were transformed into mobile palaces.

Two Portuguese fanatics, meanwhile, once drove their Transit motorhome to establish a record for the most countries visited on a single trip – 173 countries in 20 months. Now, Auto-Trail's new Transit-based Tribute T620 was declared Motorhome of the Year for 2010 by *Practical Motorhome* magazine.

The Ford Transit is now available in some 600 iterations, including the ultra-economical Econetic specification and the boy-racer Sport Van with alloy wheels. With an awe-inspiring 2.1 million sold in Britain since 1965, it holds the astounding record of having been the nation's best-selling light-commercial vehicle in its class every single year since introduction in 1965. And, yes, 93% of Transits sold today are indeed white ones. . . .

A fitting tailpiece of the earliest and latest Transits – the Ford van has been the British bestseller in its class for an astonishing 45 years.